BAC

Backwork

ANN DRYSDALE

PETERLOO POETS

First published in 2002
by Peterloo Poets
The Old Chapel, Sand Lane, Calstock, Cornwall PL18 9QX, U.K.

A catalogue record for this book is available
from the British Library

ISBN   1-904324-00-2

Printed in Great Britain By
Antony Rowe Ltd, Chippenham, Wilts.

ACKNOWLEDGEMENTS

Thanks are due to the editors of the following, in which several of the poems in this volume first appeared: *Envoi, Equinox, News That Stays News, Red Poets Number Seven* and *City Lights*.

"Darren" won fourth prize in the Cardiff International Poetry Competition in 1997 and "Going Light" won third prize in the Manchester Competition in the same year. "Misremembering Green" was a co-winner of the second prize in the 1999 Housman Society competition, in which "Imbolc" was also highly commended. "New Fruit" won second prize in the 2002 National Poetry Competition.

"Ninety-nine" was illustrated by artist Lorna Lloyd and formed part of a poetry calendar she produced at the University of Wales (Newport).

south west arts

Cui dono lepidum novum libellum
Arido modo pumice expolitum? ...

Catullus

Contents

Page

9   The Only Road There Is
10   Backwork
11   Miaow, There Goes Mr. Brown
12   Helen Goes Through
13   White Goods
14   Adult Education
15   Watching The Perseids
16   Active Listening
18   Sumimasen
19   Friday
20   Goodnight
21   Since You Ask…
22   Identity Parade
23   Ninety-nine
24   Rott's Pendulum
25   The Story-Ball Amoeba
26   Boot Hill
27   Eggshell
28   Waiting to Sign On
30   Jobclub
31   Town of Books
32   Signed Copy
33   Imbolc
34   Misremembering Green
35   The Touching-tree
36   Palliative Procedures
36   1. GOING LIGHT
37   2. PROGNOSIS
38   3. WHAT NOW
39   4. WILL IT BE LIKE THIS
40   5. DOING WITHOUT DOLPHINS
42   6. STAGE FRIGHT
43   7. THE SHADOW OF THE MOON
44   8. THE ROAD TO RECOVERY

45   Act of Worship
46   Whistlespit
47   Shibboleth
48   Welsh Now
50   Wellydancing
52   Landslip
54   The Pissing Cow
55   Darren
56   Marian
57   Foxy Lady
58   Rachel's Marmalade
59   Gran Visits
60   Two Ways of Looking at a Black Bird
61   Raven
62   Ground Crew
64   Loss Of Swifts
65   The Guinea Fowl
66   Making Love to Elbidge
68   The Big Dog's Eggs
69   Sow
70   Sale Day at the Stud Farm
71   Gathering Frogs
72   The Song of Dun Karm's Canary
74   Æthra's Secret
75   Walnut
76   Keiko's Gift
77   Handling Shit
78   Keeping it Clean
80   Little Room
81   Against Rhyming
82   Double Dactyl
83   Riverstation
84   Lines to a Gentleman
85   From the Heart
86   The Self I Made You
87   New Fruit

The Only Road There Is

When the midwife slaps our arses and initiates our clocks,
She starts us on our journey from the hard place to the rocks
And off we go like billy-oh, our little legs a blur,
Until we reach the finish and we're back to where we were.
It's a really rotten swindle, it's a monumental chizz;
We can't believe it's happening although we know it is.
We are on the road to nowhere, we are riding for a fall,
We are dying, Egypt, dying. O God! O Montreal!
We start by asking questions in the flowering of our youth
And try disguising ancient lies as universal truth.
We look at things in mirrors and we practise to deceive
And since we're only human and we're eager to believe
That we deserve a better way than all before have trod,
We go in search of holy men to broker deals with God.
We do the things they tell us in a wild desire to please;
We read the words that comfort us as though they're recipes
And serve up variations in an individual size,
Like "Rosebud", "Bugger Bognor" and "Bellamy's veal pies".

Backwork

One would prefer, on reflection, not to be at the cutting edge.
There is a fundamental unsafety in sharp tools.

The first stab into the unsuspecting, the bold slash,
The first step over the top with the quivering falchion
Slicing the still air in advance of me.
No, thank you.

In the shady world of the worker underground
There are already enough hackers and slashers
To drive forward the boundaries of invention,
Making small holes in the hitherto unknown and
Leaving it lying in lumps on the ground around them.

But up ahead, at the place where it all happens,
In the occasional hush between snapping of snap tins,
You may hear the sound of a soft, dedicated scraping.

Is it a rat, colonising a worked-out seam?
No. Me. Working close to my chest with a bastard file.

Backwork: a mining term. Work done underground but not at the coalface.
Bastard file: a file with teeth of a medium degree of coarseness.

Miaow, There Goes Mr. Brown

*Dedicated to the critic who pooh-poohed a poet's description of an
old tom cat "slinking like sewage", saying that the simile added nothing
to the picture, on the grounds that "sewage does not slink".*

People who tinker similes for a living
Test them like pots; they listen carefully
To see whether they strike the proper note
And then they turn them up the other way
To see if they hold water.

Once, underground, researching for a piece
On others' occupations, I walked tall
And carefully along a narrow channel
That carried waste from somewhere to the sea.
I learned the lingo. Rags are dirty debris
That clogs the sides of pipes; the real curse
Of menstruation. Spiral cascades take
Things – out of body out of mind – whizzing
Through flumes and bouncing down stone steps, speeding
The maceration of lumps. My companions,
Who loved and understood their plashy world,
Guided me gently through the truth of it.
One of them drew me suddenly aside
With 'Whoops, my flower!   Here comes Mr.Brown!"

A corky orange turd bobbed in the stream.
Reaching the aggregation of wellingtons
Interrupting the flow, it changed direction;
Transformed into a ginger fugitive,
An old tom cat avoiding confrontation,
It slunk past in the shadow of the wall.

Helen Goes Through

Today my sister Helen is Going Through.
Turning her face indoors and thrusting forward,
Fanatical rictus turned on the placid dirt.

This is a zealot's cleansing; a lone jihad.
She carries the battle first to the latrine,
Giving it socks and what-for with neat bleach.

Now like a gentle Jain she sweeps before her
So that she shall not step on the unsuspecting,
Sparing all small lost parts and Lego bricks.

And now like Jehu, driving her throbbing chariot
To and fro over the sacrificial pile
Sucking up all that cannot hold its ground.

Nephews are hiding outside, only returning
Under the cover of watertight excuses
One at a time to see if the coast is clear.

See them peeping through clouds of panicking dustmotes
At this object both of devotion and of sacrifice
Cutting her swathe. Jagannath, Going Through.

White Goods

It is hiding, lying in wait in the empty house;
Strip-light susurrus, refrigerator whine,
Slow, laboured breathing of the chesty freezer,
All the collective sighing of devices.

Was it like this for Abishag the Shunammite?
Did she ever squat at the foot of the king's bed
Blowing gobbets of fluff in the stale air, nothing to do
But listen to the cacophonous undertones
Of sleeping power?

And did she fantasise how easy it would be
To switch it off?

Adult Education

Yoga for Ladies. 7.30 in the gymnasium

"Nobody watches anybody else", they said;
"Yoga is non-judgmental". All the same
They told me when I didn't get it right.

The swami, dark, moustachioed, overmuscled,
Accounts for such a high attendance rate:
"Now we shall do the breathing exercise
"So those of you who haven't been before
"Had better sit and watch" and so I did.

And now I see why they call him "The Peacock".
Standing with shoulders back and buttocks taut
So as to maximise his thrusting cluster
While twenty women, panting on their knees,
Tricked into the willing-bitch position,
Look up at him, holding their haunches high,
Breathing in urgent stutters: "Ralph, Ralph, Ralph"
As he struts among them on the balls of his feet.

So Dushahsana, when Shakuni's dice fell,
Tugged at the decency of Draupadi
To no avail, yet here at Ralph's command
A score of housewives make themselves obscene
And the Lord Krishna does not intervene.

Watching the Perseids

The forecast predicted no cloud from sunset to sunrise.
Perfect conditions for seeing them, everyone said.

It was his idea to stay up and watch in the garden.
"We could have soup" he suggested, "and take it outside".

But when she turned up at dusk with the soup at the ready
He was already outside, watching. Alone.

"Not for me, thank you" he said, brisk, without looking
And moved away from her silently into the dark.

But she, smiling, believed he had only forgotten
And stumbled along in pursuit with the soup in her hand.

It hurt when he turned and struck with a voice like venom
Convincing her instantly that he wished her away

And the greatest mystery left on the night of the Perseids
Was not the showers of light from the edge of the galaxy

But the puzzle of where so much anger and hate could have come from
In the time it took her to warm up a small tin of soup

Active Listening

They teach people how to listen nowadays
As part of Team Development or
Empowering the Workforce or
Fostering Creativity or
Managing Change or
Getting to Yes.

But why am I telling you this when I know that you know.

You've read the books. You believe that gently mirroring
My actions will suggest empathy. That a wide-eyed meeting
Of my flickering gaze will give me signals of interest
And that your leaning forward will give me the cue to continue.
You have learned a lot out of books so I am surprised
That you have never yet asked me "how does that make you *feel?*"
But I'll tell you anyway, Sunshine, just for the record.

Do you remember tripe?
In the days when butchers could be bothered with
The less favoured areas of domestic creatures
And liver and lights lay alongside chaps and chitterlings
To be had for a few pence by the honest poor,
Tripe was a staple of the working man, who poached it with onions.

Tripe is the lining of a beast's paunch, white and wet
And covered with rough plush. The butcher hefted soft lumps
In his big chapped hands. It slid slow from the scale-pan
Rippling over the rim onto the greaseproof with a slick plop,
Settling sappy and flat till he gathered and wrapped it.

That's how my stomach feels, sliding suddenly downwards
To land with a bare-arse slap and a sickening spread
When I see your face fold into listening mode.
You lean forward and raise an eyebrow. Supercilious.
Mocking and mirroring – *mmmmm* – while your real self
Steps backwards and sideways and, rolling its eyes to heaven,
Says clearly *Shut the fuck up, you boring clown.*

If you really want to hear what I have to say
You could always just listen to me. Passively.

Sumimasen *

An apology for saying sorry

I can't remember what it was I said;
Only that it had been a launching pad
For a projected conversation on
A subject entirely of my own choosing.

My timing was at fault. After a pause
During which you continued wiping dishes
You walked away from me to hang the cloth,
Saying "that's all right, then". And I said "Sorry".

How else should one acknowledge a rebuke?
You had honed your consonants into sharp points
And pushed them home with slick enunciation:
I had transgressed, I stung and I was sorry.

That's all there was to it. No major deal.
But you said briskly "don't apologise"
As though you minded my having said "sorry"
And made me feel like saying it again.

But that's just me; I would apologise
To a hedgehog if I stepped on it inadvertently.
Barefoot. Sorry.

*A Japanese expression for "sorry-without-end";
a state of perpetual apology.*

Friday

The print of a bare foot, the second toe
A little longer than the one which is
Traditionally designated "great".
Praxiteles would have admired it.

You must have left in haste; your last wet step
Before boarding your suit and setting sail,
Outlined in talcum on the bathroom floor
Mocks your habitual fastidiousness.

There is no tide here to obliterate
Your oversight. Unless I wipe or sweep
Or suck it up, it will not go away.
The thought delights me. I will keep the footprint.

Too slight, too simply human to be called
Token or promise; I am keeping it
Because it is a precious evidence
That on this island I am not alone.

Goodnight

We have wished each other a staid goodnight,
Followed the rituals of the years' devising,
Switched out the lights almost in synchrony
And turned our two heads each from the other
As a prelude to our separate journeys.

Now as I incline mine at a slight angle
On the unyielding orthopaedic pillow
I feel the day's busy juices cooling
Like the dregs of an undistinguished soup
Mustered in an artfully-tilted plate.

If I were to dip a straw in and suck
It would disappear satisfyingly;
I choose instead to give my head a shake
like an Athenian winecup, writing
Your name, love, with whatever's left in it.

Since you ask...

Mean beads of snow come horizontal on a thin wind
that fingers the gap between wall and window frame,
flutters the edge of the wallpaper in the reveal
making it mutter and moan.

Tiny ice-wheels trundle along the tyre-tracks
till it palls and they all collapse in a rapturous heap
into the waiting hollow of the worn front step
and some creep quietly in under the door.

All day along the road rang the song of the shovels
finding the floor under the new carpet's high pile
while their dark marks quickly filled with the sky's trying
and tonight the white lies triumphant.

And I lie high on a pile of tired feathers
breathing fantastic patterns onto the window
through a nose lying low under the edge of the duvet
not caring much how the weather is with you.

Identity Parade

He was number six. I could have pointed him out
As soon as I entered the room, but the sergeant said not;
"Walk up and down and take a good look at them all
Or his lawyer will say in court we put words in your mouth".

He was number six, without a shadow of doubt,
Though he'd balanced his face on top of a long tweed coat
Which dawdled down to the tops of two hobnailed boots;
The decorous Sunday best of a farmer's son.

He was number six and I said so. They wrote it down.
They charged him with breaking and entering and assault.
But someone came round from the station to see me later
And say they were sorry, it "wasn't worth taking to court".

He was number six and guilty as hell, but he won;
His father swore he was home on the night in question.
He got away with stealing my self and my safety
And left me my name on a page, and my age (in brackets).

He was number six. He still is; while I have become
One of the anonymous women whom smart lads rob
And no more real than the shadow that wakes me sometimes,
Putting a face on the shape of a noise in the night.

...And the chair-leg under his anorak looks like a gun
  And his off-white socks have turned his hands into paws
  And I stare at his knobbly, naked immaculate ankles
  In the ugly shoes that are signed with the name of Victory...

Ninety-nine

Ninety-nine was the number on Gran's privy door,
Made from two disparate sixes, upside-down
In a ring of bottle-tops. Gran wasted not.
At school, conventional, I went to playground toilets
For a number one or a number two.
At Gran's on holiday, I had a ninety-nine
And there was almost a hundred difference.
Low porcelain, long chains, *Now Wash Your Hands*
And cold, unyielding tracing-paper wipes
Gave place to a rickety bucket with a lid
In a tin shed at the top of a cottage garden,
Newspaper squares threaded on hairy string.
The first expedition on midsummer mornings
Was a tip-toe trek over dewy daisies
To sit enthroned in number ninety-nine,
The door propped open with a mossy brick,
Seeing the sun poke slow over the fens
To fondle the ginger cat under the asters;
Hearing the hot trickle rumble into the bucket
To an improvised accompaniment of larks.

Rott's Pendulum

I was in *Techniquest*, my palms tingling
From rubbing the rim of a big bronze bowl
Full of dirty water, trying to make
Resonances that would sing through it
And make its wet heart leap into the air.

I started thinking glumly about life
And how it's really all about control;
A single-minded searching for the note
That makes the water jump. We seem to be
Ill-at-ease with the unfathomable.

Rott's Pendulum hung limp in its glass case.
It demonstrated human impotence.
One pendulum suspended from another;
The one gave the illusion of control,
The other behaved with perverse free will,
Quite random, wholly unpredictable.
I had a go; as soon as I touched it
I knew that I had done this thing before:
My hands were familiar with the slow wind,
The wait, the second-guessing – *will it, won't it?*
The exquisite pause between *Whoops!* and *Wheeeee!*

I had a toy that gave me my first taste
Of that almost erogenous delight.
My little Mickey Mouse, my *Disney Dancer*.
I turned him slowly on a wheel until
He flicked his skinny little legs aloft;
Most of him answered to my dull thumbs' winding
But wild shins dangled loose from his hinged knees
And yellow boots kicked over logic's traces
Into the freedom at the heart of Chaos.

The Story-Ball Amoeba

I was telling you a story,
A true rendering of a true event,
Making it for you as I went along,
Crafting it in response to your reactions
Like a cook dripping water into pastry.

Perhaps I put in a little too much at once
Or stirred too hard: you made a sudden move,
Twisted my growing story out of my hands,
Started to pull it hopelessly out of shape.

It softened, a pseudopodium oozing out
From a perfectly presentable amoeba
Making it peaky and thin.
Suddenly there was a whole new nucleus;
Extruded protoplasm gave in and let go.

It was my ball; I was playing with it.
I didn't even throw it in your direction.
You snatched it from me and stood stotting it
In front of me, but just out of my reach.

I lost control of the game. You moved the goalposts.
You tucked the ball under your arm and ran with it.
The new amoeba laid claim to its own space.
I scraped what was left of the pastry into the bin.

You left me wondering all over again
About the integrity of the oral tradition.

Boot Hill

There is a hill near Blaenau Ffestiniog, made
of the remains of thousands of pairs of boots
destroyed just after World War II

I burned a pair of boots once. I can remember
I threw them one at a time on the back of the fire.
They were old, used boots. In true Yorkshire tradition
I had worn them for weeks after they were done for,
Keeping my new ones until there was dust on the box
And the final burning was more of a rite of passage
Than a casting-away of old boots, of old friends.

I remember the smell, the black smoke as the soles melted,
The spit-and-sizzle as they turned to boiling tar
And dripped loud and stinking between the chuckling coals.
And then the slow catching of the dead leather,
The burst of applauding flame as it let itself go.

And on the next day, when it was cold, and over,
Taking the poker and riddling the black, crisp crust
Till the eyelets tinkled one by one through the grating.
Carrying transfigured remains to the bin on a shovel.
There is rather a lot left after you've burned a boot.

But a hill of boots! It must have lit up the country
Like a great beacon to celebrate once-and-forever
And the smoke must have hung in the sky like disappointment
When the fire had gone and would not come again.

Eggshell

This is the Job Centre, where I sign on
Briefly, at miserable intervals.
It is a little block of offices
Set into another, larger building;
As it were, a stiff little accident,
A ganglion, a coprolite in shale.

It is wrapped round with a hypermarket
That sells ephemera to the impecunious,
Persuading them they want the sorry tat
By demonstrating that they can afford it.
Tuneless windchimes and little lamps for burning
The cheap oil that comes in a dozen colours
And all of them with the same whorehouse smell.
Ill-finished gloves that stretch to fit all sizes,
Blinds made of sewn-together plastic straws
Knocked out in sweatshops half a world away
And sold as add-ons to the silly lives
Of people confused as to the nature
Of quality.
              Today, behind the store
A don't-care driver had let fall a box
Of Christmas baubles. One of them had rolled
Half-heartedly up to the Job Centre.
It lay broken open in the gutter,
Its white inside, naked and vulnerable,
Suggested an egg fallen from a nest
But the glitter-rough gold of its outside
Spattered with silver stars and girdled round
With crimson rings like an angry planet
Sent me smiling away, leaving it there
Hoping some fellow signer-on might see it
And have a little grin, imagining
The bird that might have laid it.

27

Waiting to Sign On

When we were very young our jobs were done
In potties, to rounds of adult applause.
Jobs done at the right time, in the right place,
Were suitably rewarded. In such soil
The Protestant work ethic germinated
And jobs done otherwhere or not at all
Were little milestones on the road to Hell.

The same attitude is apparent here
Where those without employment come to make
Their regular excuses. *No, not yet.*
I have done everything that you suggest
But had no luck so far. I'm really sorry.
And cap in hand we shuffle to the desk
To sign our little testaments of failure.

The ambience conspires to convince us
Our failure to perform is our own fault.
We are not giving out what is expected of us.
We are furballs in the innards of society.
We could all do jobs if we could be bothered
To straighten up and fly right. We're not trying
Hard enough. Not pushing. Not concentrating.

No longer a matter of self-esteem
Or of gainful employment; Job just is.
A word that doesn't stand for anything.
It bears no relation to skill or aptitude.
It has been bandied back and forth until
Its shades of meaning have been worn away
By constant successions of sweaty hands.

Here Job is once more what it used to be.
The word drops audibly from time to time
Breaking the surfaces of conversations
That trickle anonymously behind closed doors.
Stand in the queue and listen. You will hear it
Plopping disconsolately at random intervals –
Job. Job-job-job. Job. Job.

Jobclub

I have been here before in another life.
Then it was lonely hearts who gathered
In a puddle of hope around the dating agency,
Clinging together because of what they lacked
And all steadfastly denying the blindingly obvious;
That all stood a better chance if we hunted alone.

People with a common need should be spread thin
Like vanishing cream over the face of things
And rubbed in gently until they are absorbed.
To gather together so many incomplete people
In single-minded pursuit of the same missing piece
Feels like a celebration of despair.

The room is always dark. Long ranks of trestles
Underline high, dim windows. The sort of faces
That win prizes for detached photographers
Half turn as I enter. My composition soles
Fart on the linoleum. The small blonde woman
With the child's haircut, registered disabled,
Conducts her customary one-woman show.

God, if it be Thy will, grant that I love these people.
Forgive my middle class self-righteousness.
Let me accept that I am one of them
And that being here is the price of failure.

Town of Books

For R B *on the occasion of his coronation*

Here we go gathering books in Hay, books in Hay, books in Hay
Here we go gathering books in Hay on a cold and frosty morning...

Being a bound volume in the Town of Books
Is not necessarily safe or comfortable.

> *He who leaves his books outdoors*
> *Is on a par with sluts and whores*

Books by the yard, books by the pound,
"How many can you cram into a bag?"

> *He who leaves them in the rain*
> *Causes poor Saint Peter pain*

They are brought here, sought and bought here,
Priced but not valued, wanted but not loved.

> *To pile them high and sell them cheap*
> *Makes recording angels weep*

Alas for the bright books, brought low and traded
Into all sorts of slavery, all manner of mischief.

Signed Copy

There it was, in the Poetry Bookshop,
Flagrantly overpriced; who in their right mind
Would pay fifteen quid for a five pound book?

Not even out of print, as I well know
Because I'd recently had cause to ask,
This volume being one I hadn't got.

But you had signed it fifteen years ago
To J, specifically, with your love
And admiration, which had raised its value.

It was a book I wanted, but the price
Was more than I had ever meant to pay.
Nevertheless I took it home with me.

Five pounds bought the book, and the other ten
Bought the small secret that I shall keep close
And proudly, to protect you from it.

So you shall never know J or her heirs
No longer have the book, the admiration
Or the love you gave with it, years ago.

I'll keep it safely, with more recent books
That you have signed for me. A little kindness
In token of my love and admiration.

Imbolc

In November I took issue with the privet,
Challenging its entitlement to so much sky
When the other shrubs could do with a bit of it.

November is the time of dying, of Samhain;
It is the start of darkness. It was a dark act
When I tore out the living heart of the old bush.

I left scars, and nothing came to make them better
Because the year was dead, too, and beyond giving;
I was left looking a long time at what I'd done.

And the debris lay the length of the waiting-time;
The mean days, short and brittle, the annual sulk
That makes a lying-in-state between slash and burn.

Now I felt it was time to put an end to it;
I built a pyramid pyre of the dead privet
Round screwed-up newspaper and put a match to it.

But it burned grudgingly, squeezing a thin grey smoke
Out of its entrails, while a threadbare shawl of rain
Wrapped itself round it like an asbestos blanket .

So I re-framed the situation, told myself
That fire for fire's sake was not the thing that mattered;
It was the thought that counted, the blind act of faith.

Midnight. A squall scuttering along the valley
Blows on the cold ashes, filling the sky with fire.
The wake is over; now the waking can begin.

Misremembering Green

This is how it begins, a sort of taking for granted,
A daily conviction that this is as green as it gets
And soon it will turn on its heel and go spinning downhill.

Each spring the smile starts as the first smug buds
Pop out like pustules on the face of the bare wood,
Stretching one at a time into little leaves.

All the time telling myself, just wait until summer,
Warning myself not to miss it, under-expecting
And being as always taken by surprise.

Finding I had forgotten the sheer bulk of it
All those top-heavy towerings of honeysuckle
Mocking the memory of my tentative pruning.

Green foam extruding steadily under pressure,
Knobbling from unsuspected interstices,
Shape-shifting into viridescent dunes.

Unstoppable swellings on familiar faces,
Filling the gaps around ill-fitting windows
Of opportunity for their self-advancement.

And me standing still in the awful silence of it
Promising myself that this time I will remember
While knowing that as always I shall forget

The Touching-tree

Today they felled the touching-tree
Which stood between the town and me.
I wasn't there. I didn't see.

Not my town. Not my tree.
I touched it surreptitiously.
A finger-kiss as I went by,
With nobody aware but I
Of what I did to it. And why.

An exquisite simplicity.
Keeping a promise to a tree
Made sure the world was safe for me.
A little unobtrusive act.
A sign of faith. A private pact.

If someone else was there with me
I never used to touch the tree
Or talk about the need to touch;
It seemed to matter far too much.
Next time I passed I touched it twice.
Act of contrition. Sacrifice.

It was substantial, safe and tall.
And now there's nothing there at all.
Only the marks of boots and tyres
And grappling hooks and straining wires
And sawdust.

No mighty willow any more.
Only the fear I touched it for.

Palliative Procedures

1. GOING LIGHT

They call it "going light", the loss of substance
That goes with the failing of the spirit
When the end comes.

My old dog went light just before he died.
His thin bones whispered in his hairy skin
And went to sleep

And all that was left of him was the light
That faded slowly as his eyes went dim;
The other light.

Going light, light going. It was as if
I had perceived a sort of sense in it
For a moment.

Two kinds of light, making an hourglass
Laid on its side between weight and darkness;
The shape of dying.

Death is the snapping of the narrow neck
In between substance and oblivion
And that is all.

And as you come near to the glass isthmus
I wish for the breaking to be gentle.
Go light, my love.

2.PROGNOSIS

It was done quickly. Just a small, clean cut;
it hardly bled at all, and anyway
they had the dressings ready, laid them on
before we got a look at what had happened.

At first we only saw the analgesic
messages written on the clean, white gauze:
Statistics lie. It may not grow at all.
Or not for some considerable time.
There are techniques being developed now...
Surgeons in Cardiff... Surgeons in Birmingham...

When we got home we soaked it in warm water
to ease a growing ache and, one by one,
the dressings floated off. *Buts* drifted loose
and echoed... *given your history...*
due to your age... Assertions came to bits
and lay limp in the bottom of the bowl
as it all sunk in.

I fished out the damp dressings. Useless now,
for none of them would stick back on again.
Only the cold mischief of statistics
had any mileage left in it and so
here we are holding hands across the wound,
feeling it all slipping away, clutching
at randoms, variables and the tails of curves.

3. WHAT NOW?

When the ground opened up in front of me
I did what I did almost without thinking.

The situation called for sacrifice
And, like the old Roman, I plunged in.

I hit the bottom hard, but I'm OK;
Nothing is broken and I can still breathe

After a fashion. Little sips of air
Visit my hungry lungs in fits and starts;

I've not yet dared to draw one of them down
Any deeper. My stomach's still falling.

Everything has gone quiet, settled down
Into a sort of sad resignation.

I don't regret the leap, but something's wrong.
This isn't how it was supposed to be.

It's very cold and very dark down here
But when I look up, I can still see sky.

The old Roman: Mettus Curtius. In 362 BC a chasm appeared in the middle of the Roman forum and soothsayers said it could only be filled by throwing in the city's greatest treasure. Mettus Curtius put on his armour, mounted his horse, rode full tilt at the crack and leaped in. The earth closed over him.

4. WILL IT BE LIKE THIS?

Looking to my left, I could see clearly
The curve of your cheek, the light-coloured bulge
Where your shoulder made a shelf for it.

Nearer, your ear, with the unruly fuzz
Of your jowl throwing its perfect outer curve
Into sweet relief against your pillow.

But as I moved to press my morning smile
Into the curve of your neck, I found nothing
But foam and linen, nothing but bedding.

The cheek was sheet, the shoulder naked pillow
Squeezing out of its shrunken envelope,
The ear the swelling round a quilting button.

Panic then, and loss until I found you,
Slid further down, breathing sweet and heavy
In the deep sleep of the late-lying sluggard.

Relief came, and I lay looking for laughter
In the silliness of what had just happened,
But there was only a small, cold question.

Will it be like this when you-know-what happens?
Will I still wake to you when you're not there?
Will I still look for you? Will it be like this?

5. DOING WITHOUT DOLPHINS

Hospice Clinic. October 2000

Persuaded here against my better judgement,
feeling the oil-and-crystal ambience,
lying alert and still.

"I swim with dolphins" says the massage lady,
"it is a mystical experience".

Prone on the table, through a face-shaped hole
watching my own fists clenching into knots,
thinking – *what if my hands could see my face?*
All jowls and eyebags, slowly dripping down
to form a nightmare physiognomy –
a winner in a gurning competition ......

I try to share this with the massage lady:
"Do you know gurning?" "No", she says and then
returns deftly to the subject of dolphins.
"They are so good, such spiritual beings;
"one knows they know the secrets of the soul
"and how to heal it....."

Her little stroking hands; my tired flesh
shuddering under their ministrations,
my head fighting to bring disparate worlds
to an accommodation.

Spirituality is not my thing
but stretched out at the mercy of a stranger
I did experience a small epiphany.

Some put their faith in dolphins; some cannot.
Somebody who fine-tunes her view of life
by mugging at it through a toilet seat
does not escape responsibility.

I'll seek alternative alternatives,
working on ways of mending what is broken
which do not call for the participation
of dolphins.

6. STAGE FRIGHT

Living with dying takes a bit of doing.
It's rather like rehearsing for a play;
I'm working on the words, watching the cueing
So as to do the business come the day.
Mine's a supporting role; it's not my show –
I can't direct the action from onstage.
It's hard to pace myself when I don't know
Whether or not we're on the closing page.
I know I'll manage when push comes to shove -
I've never doubted that the final curtain
Ought to be improvised out of our love;
It's getting there that isn't quite so certain.
The question isn't if I can be strong,
It's if I can be this afraid that long.

7. THE SHADOW OF THE MOON

"Oh, what the hell" we said, and did the thing
Without protection. Risky undertaking.
With our bare eyes we watched the sun's eclipse
Reflected in the surface of the pond.

Wet-blanket clouds had shackled its full power;
It lay in the water, Achilles' shield,
Dull, sunken silver. Then a dozen ide –
Pond-swallows – gurgitated centre-stage
Chasing a drift of midges, shattering
The picture beyond mere representation –
Matisse – Cézanne – and all the broken light
Shimmered into a glorious, soundless noise.

I turned to you to share the glee, and saw
The first shadow of pain crossing your face.
You hid it well. No sooner there than gone.

The cloud lifted. The sun was back again.
The ide retreated into the dark place
Under the lilies. Something had ended.
Something had begun.

8. THE ROAD TO RECOVERY

There is no us any more; I have lost you.
This is where it begins, the slowly road
That will take me away from here to where
I can begin again.

The first step is the hardest, so they say.
In the light of this I forgive myself
A desultory dawdle on the doorstep,
A long look back inside.

I slam the fucking door. It's so unfair!
Why should I have to handle all this shit?
I didn't think you'd ever bugger off.
Christ, I don't need this!

I walk a little way. Halfhearted drizzle
Makes my clothes heavy. I want to turn back.
I could have handled so much of it better
And cry to try again.

I creep under the hedge, lie in the dry
With lords-and-ladies, stinking phalluses
And such. From here I watch the world go by –
All shoes and socks and ankles.

A tentative finger of thin sun
Pokes slowly into the mulch. I come out
All covered in crap like a spring hedgehog
Blinking in disbelief.

And here I am. At the end of the road.
Recovered. And the door in front of me
Opens. Look! There is no us any more.
I have lost you.

Act of Worship

My own house is a holy place for my purposes;
my pottering in it is a sort of prayer.

By making the effort to come home
I have turned my back on all the fidgety busyness
of the sticky world I spun around myself, its plan
no longer entirely recognisable. A sad old spider
whose knitting feet fumble forgotten patterns,
I wander unwatched, forgiving myself slowly.

Forgiving myself for the terrible lapse of taste
That put the stained glass in the door – *my dear, so* **thirties!**
Forgiving the blowsy bevels because of the rainbows
coincidentally blessing the dizzy dust.

Becoming slowly glad, recalling the slick, sweet taste
of the safety that lives in the dark behind closed doors.
The dear curves of the squat little armchair, the benison
bestowed unconditionally on the backs of bare knees
by the kiss of uncut moquette.

These are my own things. Nobody else would want them,
yet among them I can give thanks; here I can praise.
I am home again, after a long time; a lapsed Catholic
absentmindedly making all the appropriate gestures,
prompted by long-forgotten habit.

For it feels like being in church, the afternoon ending
in a fine, slow, aromatic contemplation,
an old cat limp in my lap like a Sunday glove.

Whistlespit

To Jenny Galton-Fenzi

Although I try to make the best of it
There are two reasons why I hate it here;
The old men whistle and the young men spit.

The olds don't make a decent fist of it;
It's not a proper whistle, sharp and clear,
Although I know they do their best with it.

They suck in air, blow it about a bit,
Take pot shots at a tune; get nowhere near.
Thus old men whistle. And the young men spit –

Though that's a poor way of describing it –
Great yellow gleaming gobs. I live in fear
Although I try to make the best of it.

Do you begin to catch the drift of it?
The young offend the eye, the old the ear;
The old men whistle and the young men spit.

I jest a bit to give the gist of it,
Just so you get the general idea:
Although I try to make the best of it –
The old men whistle and the young men spit.

Shibboleth

The coach-works in Bradford are known far and wide,
A centre of excellence, really,
For turning vehicular fiction to fact
If requirements are specified clearly.

We'd a bloody great order not too long ago –
A bit of a triumph for Sales –
For twenty-four buses, done inside and out,
For a private contractor in Wales.

The seats were all covered in quality twill;
The exteriors shone like a dream
In Verona (a sort of a special dark green)
And Buttermilk (up-market cream).

We'd almost accomplished best part of the job
And the paintwork were gleaming and grand
Wi' twelve coats all over, sprayed on in the shop
And the coachlines all finished by hand.

There were customised logos; two dragons per bus,
Which were done in a Post Office Red,
But we had no instructions for painting the words
So we rang them to see what they said.

"We don't want to spoil a spectacular job
So we thought we'd refer it to you –
Do you want this here *kim-roo* Verona or Gold –
And will next week delivery do?"

"The word should be *Cymru*" the customer said
With a hint of a taste of a sneer.
So we sent 'em back painted C-U-M-R-Y
'cause that's how we spell *Cymru* round here.

Welsh Now

By and by is easily said
Shakespeare, *Hamlet.*

When English overlords overran Wales
They brutalised the menfolk, used the women
And frightened schoolchildren into submission.
If the poor mites dared speak in their own tongue
A wooden notice was hung round their necks
Bearing the terrible legend "Welsh Not"
(Pokerwork, probably, the atrocity
Happily pre-dating the felt-tip pen).
All who are not Welsh know about "Welsh Not"
Because Welsh people tell them.

Perhaps if things had gone the other way
We'd have had an English equivalent.
Small Saxons might have worn it scornfully
Or drawn two fingers on the other side
And worn it back to front. But not the Welsh.
The Welsh bear grudges for a long time
And saying sorry doesn't help. I've tried.
All I can do is note your small revenge
And bravely let you get away with it.

For now you hurt me where I once hurt you:
You have stolen from me my English 'now',
My instantaneous, my immediate,
And given me instead another 'now' –
Your now-and-again, your now-in-a-minute
To remind me of the longstanding debt.
I do not like it, but I understand.

I am a proud Sais and it ill becomes me
To be reduced to the role of beggar,
But please, when you say "I will do it now",
Give me some token – a small wooden plaque
Would be ideal. I'd hang it round my neck
As a reminder, lest I should forget
That you have awarded me the "Welsh Now".
Even though I have long since forgotten
What I was waiting for.

Wellydancing

"It was incumbent upon us to dance
Each time we heard the strains of Barwick Green."

Over the years I grew to hate *The Archers*.
They represented the brass face of farming
That mooned down disdainful upon the peasant
Whose business was merely a way of life.

After a stint from dawn till dusk outdoors
The first notes of the smug signature tune
Would launch me angrily across the kitchen
To distance myself from them by applying
Swift pressure to the appropriate tit.
This unnerved the children, but I told them
That just as we'd switch off *God Save the Queen*
So as to avoid standing to attention,
I squelched this so as not to have to dance.

Then they found ways to make it otherwise,
Preventing me from switching off *The Archers*
So that I stuck my fingers in my ears
And danced dirty in the unkempt kitchen,
Rubber boots slapping on the cold, flagged floor,
Miming the anguish of a goaded bear
While three triumphant children giggled bells
Until our grim and grubby world exploded
Into gaiety while the music lasted.

They told sophisticated visitors
"Don't let our mother switch *The Archers* off
until you've seen her do the welly dance."

All that was a very long time ago
And I have folded and put by such things.

But still it sometimes takes me unawares:

> *Archers!* Muezzin-call. Cathedral bells.
> An undeniable imperative.
> And I, all alone in a foreign land,
> Give in to the pressure of the old promise
> And, in imaginary wellingtons,
> I dance the peasant's dance of the Old Country;
> The dance of Joy and Dung and What-the-hell!

Landslip

Mynydd Carn y Cefn

It appeared suddenly, a quick rip in silk;
a green shirt tearing so as to expose
an unexpected piece of underneath.

A backscar, marking the length of a new slip,
the next instalment in the slow collapse
of the mountain on whose knee my house sits.

Over the years custodians have abused it,
piling detritus from their greedy beavering
shoulder-high into its long, green lap.

This was no way to treat so young a mountain.
In a few millennia its baby shales
might have matured and hardened into slate.

They worked it too hard, like a chimney sweep,
stealing its youth and dirtying its beauty;
scrambling its soft insides, breaking its bones.

They've tried to make amends, to kiss it better
by carting off the spoil and planting trees
but still the ground shifts and the cracks appear.

There is an outside chance the lot may go
and there is a Procedure written down
but nobody will tell me what it is.

Someone let slip that such a thing exists
and I was suddenly afraid, wondering –
if it happens, what will descend on us?

First the brown envelopes to The Occupier.
Clipboards, Confusion. Rows of pens in pockets.
I've got a job to do, love. Don't ask me!

Power of small men in big situations.
Ordering. Hectoring. Nobody listening.
Hopelessness. Impotence. Authority.

I was afraid; not of the changing face
of the mountain, but the unbending aspect
of a few little people in the valley.

Time has eroded the rough edge of terror.
The mountain smiles as the sun warms its corners
and shifts imperceptibly in its sleep.

But I still play *what I would do if the mountain fell*
because I am the sort of person I am
and because, sooner or later, the mountain will.

The Pissing Cow

For the neighbour who calls me this
behind my back, and thinks I don't know.

It is evident that you know little about cattle
Or you'd not have chosen that particular term of abuse.
Poor soul, you will never have felt on your upper lip
The natural effervescence of fresh milk

Or heard the rough music of ruminant digestion
In stereo, lying in straw between two cows.
Never watched swing-titted milkers in full sail
Distributing manurial largesse.

Piss elegant she is, the pissing cow,
Her tail curlicued like a little finger
Quivering in the cloud of fragrant steam
Rising from Earl Grey in bone china.

See the golden stream pour over the lip
Of her pouting vulva onto the soft brown saucer
That waits to catch it like a Yorkshire pudding
Calling for the kiss of gravy.

Who would not appreciate the slap and trickle
Of the artistic statement that she's making
While her companions drop their slow dung round her
In an ongoing ripple of restrained applause.

There are three things, friend, that you should learn from this:
That there is beauty in all things that are without pretension;
That a poet only gains by association with them;
That there are sadder things in life than a pissing cow.

Darren

He's a bully; I've been afraid of him
Ever since he pinned me against a wall
And threatened me with a clenched fist, saying
He'd "had enough of me", that "something would happen"
Unless I "fuck off", which is difficult
Since I was in no position to ask
His working definition of the phrase.

So I applied an educated guess
And now contrive to be where he is not.
This means I hide from him, planning my routes
So as to avoid any confrontation.
I probably walk miles out of my way
So that I do not have to pass his house
And hear his vomiting impressions
Or the great guffaws of lunatic laughter
He taunts me with if I walk past his window.

I watch him, too, from places of safety,
So as to be sure when the coast is clear.

He has a Staffordshire bull terrier
And when he takes it out for exercise
It hauls ahead of him on a taut lead
Like a metal-detector, its legs bowed
To accommodate its prodigious balls.
Darren has adopted its way of walking:
See how he struts wide-legged along the street
As though incommoded by heavy tackle.

Holding his arms a little awkwardly
Around two heavy rolls of bugger all,
He goes importantly about his business.
Darren. Delivering the Emperor's New Carpet.

Marian

We all assumed that that bloke of hers had done it
With his free and easy fists in the ebullience of booze;
Three cracked ribs that "pained her something cruel"
And we all thought we knew who the cruel something was.

Even the doctor thought the same as we did –
"Turn him in, love, he's no bloody good to you, that one".
She persisted. "It was the cough" she told him. "Honest;
He never laid a finger on me. The coughing done it."

Off to a specialist. Osteoporosis, he told her,
Can sometimes produce such results from a violent cough.
"He's a thieving, cheating bastard, but he's never hit me"
She proclaimed, triumphant. "It was the coughing done it."

I saw her this morning. Head under an umbrella
That tossed like a rutting tortoise in time with the cough.
Flicking the ash off her fag with a yellow finger –
Marian, abusing herself with a small white stick.

Foxy Lady

Eve has just been here.
Stopping at the bottom of the stone steps
To breathe before I embark on the climb
I sniff her having passed on the still air.

Evening in Paris?
Childhood comes once again into flower,
Blossoming into all the cheap perfumes
That fired my adolescent ambition.

Woolworth's after school.
June Roses. Phul Nana. Aqua Manda.
The soft, sweet reek oozing from the counters
Said I could be an object of desire.

Cloves in an orange.
Pomander. Posy clutched against the plague;
These kind scents would do what was necessary –
Hide my unfinished femininity.

In another life
I stood on a moorland track, sniffed the wind,
Drew in the rank smell that had halted me
And knew that a vixen had passed this way.

A horny bouquet.
Urine and dog-feet. Sweat of a ripe bitch
Curled up for a long time in a small space.
A calling-card with a sly suggestion.

Evening in Paris?
I sprint up the steps to catch a swift glimpse
Of short-legged Eve in her fun-fur coat
Slinking along the street. My foxy lady.

Rachel's Marmalade

Definitely unsweet; tart even.
A decidedly grown-up marmalade,
Knowing its own mind. See how firm it stands
On a toasted muffin, responding now
To the knife coaxing it towards the edge,
But only as much as is necessary.

Amber and warm; a mature marmalade.
There are pips in it, and the crusty bits
That have protected the soft fruit so far
And are the making of the taste of it.
Hold it up to the window; see the world
Perfectly clearly through its golden heart.

Rachel once said to me that she had thought
That no poet would ever celebrate her
And then felt comforted to think I might
Be moved to do it. Would she feel the same
If she could see me now, *déshabillée,*
Practising on her home-made marmalade?

Gran visits

Gran's coming. Everything subtly changes.
We gather ourselves into comfortable
And *cwtch* up to make her a little space
In what we're doing, so she can be safe
From any ongoing unpleasantness.

When she comes she brings back last time with her
And tests us on it. We have to remember
The old responses, like a catechism.
The price of getting it wrong is hurting her.
She freezes us like a self-satisfied hairdresser
Tilting her mirror to show us the backs of our heads.

It's not as if we lie to her, exactly;
We keep her posted as to what goes on
In a kind of conscience-dictated code.
Like Mark, for instance. *He's left University.*
He's started shooting up since you last saw him;
You wouldn't know him now.

It's as though all of us are on a journey
And Gran got off by mistake at the last stop.
Now she is bumping along behind the bus,
Her tiptoes scurrying over the ground we're covering
And her stiff fingers hooked over the rail,
Desperately dangling from the way we were.

Two Ways of Looking at a Black Bird

It's easy to be dismissive;
Claim it doesn't matter, or that
All the black buggers look alike.

I called them crows because the neighbours did
And they did because they always had.
Ornithology didn't come into it.

A twitcher told me the truth when I tried to tell him
About the big black bothersome birds in my chimney.
He knew they couldn't be crows, had to be jackdaws.

And the birds stood still while the words shifted around them:
Croaking and carrion, omens and eyesockets softened
At once into cheapjack, hi-jack, brassneck and guile.

Terrorist suddenly smiled and resolved into ruffian
While under the eaves young thugs became instantly urchins,
Though the scritch of their toenails sounded the same on the tiles

And I test with my tongue the delicious surprise of discovering
That suddenly knowing that all my crows are jackdaws
Really does make a difference.

Raven

He clasps the mast with a cricketer's fingers
High up among the paraphernalia
Of media coverage and mobile phones.
He attracts my attention. *Er – ahem –*
You there – 'scuse me – wassatime?

Throaty croak hinting at late nights and fag-smoke.
A young executive in a good black suit;
Too bad he slept in it. Stretching and flexing,
He is pulling it back into some semblance of shape
As we speak.

His jowl bristles.
He has not shaved today - designer stubble
Taken to unacceptable extremes; he is pushing his luck.
Now, ready as he'll ever be, he takes the plunge,
Flies on a straight steady line to the Black Mountains.

Lazily following the valley, he stays with the gradient
To the top of a long, slow loop. Then suddenly –
Aaagh, fuck! – as he realises he's on the wrong train.
A dive sideways. Trailing at arms' length umbrella, briefcase, raincoat,
He streaks for the Beacons.

Ground Crew

I think it one of summer's privileges
To walk at dusk along the terraces
Involuntarily ducking flung swifts.

Summer begins when the first spinning chakra
Slices the dark space above the stone lintel
Alternating in the air with its own image;
One in, one out. A beginner juggling knives.

It is assured when the first faint sound in the roofspace
Tells loving listeners that foetus is now chick
And chick and chick again as the voices multiply.

One day a fledgling fell.
Fat, feathered, fully equipped for flight
But not yet airworthy. It clung flat to the tarmac
Quite still, but not cowering. Whatever lay
Behind the closing eyes; blind faith, fortitude,
Was not for me to know.

I love the swifts; the fall of their little one mattered.
Restoring it to them was within my gift.
Had they despaired of it? – possibly. Passengers had.
The fat ticks, airforce blue, were quitting their positions,
Baling out of the grounded bird and running away.

I watched them. Let them go, the freeloading bastards;
Their chances of hitching a passing lift were nil.
And what might it mean to a swift, to know of their going?

Fast, fast I clattered upstairs into the bedroom,
Heaved up one broken sash, hauled down another,
Clearing myself a runway to the nest.

Faster I stumbled down, out into the street,
To cast a long shadow over the little aircraft
Which stared up at the great red face of salvation,
Hearing *"Okay – let's get this baby off the ground!"*

Loss of Swifts

I have lost them.
It is the last thing I think before sleep comes
And the first on waking.

They came back.
Meeting in the sky high above the valley
And homing in on the place they knew as theirs.

But it was not as they had left it.
A couple of passes up and down the terrace,
A look at the altered hole, the expensive nest-box
And they were gone again.

The Council put the ultimatum in writing;
It *had to be done.* Shifting the blame helps
But it doesn't stop me thinking about them, imagining,
Needing to know if their grief is as great as mine.

Over and over *mea culpa, mea maxima culpa*
While the swifts cry high in the hot air over the valley
And I sit willing them, wishing them, wanting them back.

I need to know how to tell it to start sanding down
The lump of regret standing proud of the smooth summer;
Guddling in my head for the words to make it right –

> *They were tourists, unsatisfied with the changed arrangements*
> *They have simply decided to take their custom elsewhere.*
> *You must come to terms with your having lost the contract*
> *Despite your high-profile attention to customer care...*

They will be all right. They will have found somewhere better.
They have only voted against me with their feet.
Their dear soft skinny inadequate lovable feet.

The Guinea Fowl

It was given to me as a solution
To someone else's problem, a fox having
Got into their pen and eaten the rest.

I had never seen such a bird before;
Perfectly round body, gingham-checked,
Carried carefully on tentative legs.
The tiny head with its stark, white make-up
The scarlet cheeks, the little pointy hat
Gave it the air of a bewildered clown
But I was not inclined to laugh at it.

It shunned the hen-house, roosting high at night
In the orchard, hunched back silhouetted
Against the indifferent moon.

By day it trudged the ruts, single-mindedly
Searching for the other half of itself ,
Holding a mirror to my own loneliness
Till I knew I must get a mate for it.

But to do this I needed to determine
Something basic about the bird in hand.
Asking how I might ascertain its gender
I was told – *cocks have more red on their heads.*

So now I sit looking out of the window
And, in tune with the melancholy bird
Picking its solitary way across the stack-yard,
Asking: *Than what? Than what? Than what? Than what?*

Making Love to Elbidge

The special chicken among a buttery dozen
Reared under a lamp in a wooden hatbox.
Her name is a conceit; my little joke.

Out of a love of eggs by a loathing of acronyms
She is LBJ, the Little Brown Job, Elbidge
To distinguish an otherwise indistinguishable

Warren. Hatched by the thousand for the batteries.
Anonymous fluff on trays in hot sheds.
I rescued a dozen for less than a pound apiece.

Genetically selected never to go broody,
Warrens are bred to lay and not to be laid;
To live without ever feeling a rooster's tread.

One half of a hen's brain deals with foodsearch,
The other side with safety. Somewhere between
Lies habit, ancient and ineradicable.

When Elbidge, fussy and confused from her laying,
Comes coyly close and curtseys at my feet
I bend and stroke her aromatic feathers.

I recognise the old urge and am flattered by it.
I fold my finger into a pseudobeak
And drive it hard into the back of her neck.

She reaches up, tiptoeing to my fingertouch
And I push harder, feeling her brace herself
Under my hand, squatting, spreading her wings.

I press for a moment, then release. She rises,
Shakes herself briskly, goes about her business.
I am all the cockerel she will ever know.

Our loving fulfils a need rather than a purpose;
No more than the momentary pressure of a knuckle
Shrugged off in a flurry of feathers, once a day.

The Big Dog's Eggs

Torque of a dog, curled round in a square chair.
Nominally nesting dog, occupying personal space
That she has negotiated with the ancient cushion
By dint of much scratching and turning.

She knows about eggs; she watches me fish them
Out of the warm darkness of the hen-house,
Finding by touch the new fruit under the broody
Biding its special time on bone china,

Given the slightest chance she will filch them prettily,
Carry them conscientiously in risky teeth
To a safe place where she opens them in secret
Like love-letters, savouring the slippery meat.

Dogs do not lay eggs. Both of us know this, and yet
When I see her curled, committed, on her notional nest,
When I ask her "How are you eggs today? May I feel them?"
She wriggles into a flat noisette of ecstasy
With sharp insistent bones that press my hand
Harder into the hot, dogsmelling places
Of her secret underneath.

Sow

Earthbound balloon, seeming simply a long, pink limpness
Slightly deflated, tethered to its own low legs
Coyly belying the great dead weight of itself.
But to the touch, how rough; stiff and somehow domestic;
Washleather ears slapping against a scrubbing-board
And a living gristle liberty bodice button
Sewn to a snout with more strength than a man's arm.

Sow, how did you make this tray of candied confectionery
Asleep along the length of your underneath,
New-trousseau pink, while your teats drip, drip, drip
Into the mouths of so many seemingly dead?

I could summon the signs of life, should the fancy take me
By slyly applying the touch of a tentative finger
To the breath-blown down on the dome of one hard little head.

Sale Day at the Stud Farm

Into the ring they lead another black slave.
A sweet-faced virgin, bred in captivity.
They call her Princess, holding her safe
On a soft, white rein.

Out of one long name by another, she is labelled
Assessed, paraded. Carefully shown in-hand
And steadied-still to present her best aspect.

Everything changes: the groom slips off the head-collar,
Says "Now, lads, let's see a bit of action"
And strikes at his Princess with the end of the rope
While the whole assembly cries like a hunt-kennel.
A voice made of yapping. Flapping their begatteries at her,
Crying *yahoo-hoo-hoo!*

Her owner calls from the rails and when she comes, trusting,
Thrusts powdered face and stencilled eyebrows at her,
Shooing her off so that she rears and whirls.

The painted madam turns, smiles at her clientele
As the horse-whore capers to their ugly tune –
Yahoo-hoo-hoo! Gerremoff! Show us yer tits!

I need to believe in a horse-faith;
Under the indoor black, the dusty ginger
A true black, blue-black spirit
In a fourth dimension, deep, high, beyond,
Where a real horse dances.

Gathering Frogs

I am gathering frogs in a builders' bucket.
Every year they come
Up from the valley bottom by snicket and ginnel
Heading towards the ponds where they were spawned.
They go to breed. They are unstoppable.

Some cannot wait. They shuffle, coupled,
Towards the patently unattainable. Some of them
Pope-Joan their jellied bellyful into the gutter.

Crossing Victoria Street, their chances
Plummet at an exponential rate. Cars.
Rough boys who boot them skywards.
Drunkards who hiccup and splat.
Here I come with my back bent, plucking
Soft living peaches from the tarmac,
Spiriting small souls into my bucket.

Swing low, sweet bucket; tip out the wet load
Here on the banks of the pond Jordan.
First they lie as they land. Then the water calls
And they begin to move, in their ones and twos
Lolloping forward little by little by little;
Now they begin their song, the throaty alleluias
Rising like tossed cloth caps.

Those rescued yesterday rise to the surface
Underpinning the anthem with gruff praise.
Do you hear them, Lord? Can you see them?
And are you well pleased?

The Song of Dun Karm's Canary

The priest Carmelo Psaila, better known as Dun Karm, Poet of Malta, fell foul of the church authorities and found himself living in a dingy flat in Valletta. There he wrote a poem about his pet canary and how it depended on him utterly and showed its gratitude each night by soothing his sorrow with a song he had taught it..

What, home to roost again so soon, black crow?
It seems no time at all since you went out;
Although I had my little golden head
Tucked tight under my wing, I watched you go.
Canaries peep. Like ducks.

I don't suppose you've given me a thought
Since then. Water and seeds. A page of *Il Habib*
Shoved into the bottom of the cage, then off.
Presumably assumed I'd hold the pose
Till you got back.

Now as you tell me all about your day
I will take refuge in a metaphor,
Stick my un-fingers into my non-ears
And tell you about my own.

I flew today. No sooner had your key
Turned in the lock than I sent myself soaring
Around all the balconies of Valletta,
Visiting prisoners in hanging cages.
I chinked with finches, sang in the languages
Of all the foreign songbirds in the city
Setting all their sad little spirits free.

All right – I lied. I have been here all day
Hopping and chirruping from time to time
The way we do.

You are still talking, Monsignor Psaila:
I am not listening; I am telling you
Something important but you cannot hear me.
You could fly too, black crow. It's just a matter
Of getting your head into the right position.

Too sad, old crow? What can I say to cheer you?
This little setback cannot last forever –
It's just a hiccup, a rap on the knuckles
For one of your many little arrogances.
What the world is, it is.

                    And one more thing:
That song you thought you taught me, Carmelito –
God gave it to me, while I was an egg.

Æthra's Secret

Tonight I swam with the seagod in the green gulf.
He came and called me; whistled under the window,
Gesturing hush with one of his long, thin fingers.
I went willingly into the slick, dark water.
We swam to the north shore where whispering shingle
Chuntered under our feet as we climbed to the quay
And under a hanging lamp, by a low, wet wall,
He peeled my costume off like a slippery skin,
And cradled my bare bum in both of his big hands.
Then face to face we fucked, with me sat in his lap,
A speared fish, riding astride his mighty phallus.
Without a word we went back into the water,
Swam silently side by side for the southern shore.
I lie beside Ægeus, keeping my secret;
Pressing my small round belly into the bed,
Pushing my damp smile down into the pillow.

*When Theseus of Athens was elevated by history
to the status of Hero, legend demanded that he
should have a more elevated provenance than a
mere Mum and Dad.......*

Walnut

It lies in the corner of a drawer
among an assortment of tools. A walnut.
Every so often I come across it,
take it out, hold it in my hand, enjoy
its hardness, wholeness, portability,
debate, then put it back among the chisels.

I ate its brothers green, fresh from the tree.
This one I saved to see what it would be
when it came into its strength, or didn't.

Walnut. It should be judged by what's inside.
Either a fat kernel, wholesome and sweet;
all that surprising, convoluted meat
to winkle out and crunch between the teeth,
or a pathetic puff of grey-green dust,
transient whiff of vegetable must,
fatally failed by its own shell. Brain-dead.

If all I had to do was open it
I would have known by now, but to find out
calls upon other words – crack, smash, break, split –
destruction masquerading as conclusion.
Best settle for the question, let the walnut
hold it, whole, sealed inside its wooden head.

Keiko's Gift

A guest-gift, in a rice-paper envelope.
Soft, droopy silk, khaki shading to puce.
Design of cherry-blossoms and small clouds.
Cold to the touch; hangs heavy in the hand.
Redolent of dark halls, furniture polish
And Clarice Cliff.

What is it? And how should I fold my face
For the acceptance of it? Quickly, think!
Too indiscreet to be a handkerchief;
Big enough for a headscarf or fichu
But sullen and unruly, needing knotting
For any semblance of obedience.
I dare not try it on.

Has it some religious significance?
Might I offend? Keiko pulls out her words –
This is what we call, in Japan, a Cloth;
We use it, in Japan, for Everything

Seeing that I have still not understood,
She tries a case in point. *When I was little girl*
My grandmother would make picnic. Little feast
Wrapped in a Cloth. I take. Adventure!

And now I understand. Holding the gift
Against my cheek, I thank her with a smile
Both for the Cloth and the enlightenment:
So ... children East and West grow up believing
That everything important can be gathered
Into a knotted hanky; kept forever
Tied by four corners to a good stout stick.

Handling Shit

Shit happens. Everybody gets their share;
the sorry stuff doesn't discriminate –
it hits the fan and then it's everywhere.
Nobody ducks until it's far too late.
A canny lass can never have too many
plans for confronting an emergency.
A sonnet is as good a way as any.
It did for Shagsberg; it'll do for me.
So sock it to me, Sunshine. I can take it.
I'll dredge the sludge for something new to say.
I'll squeeze the mental Plasticine and make it
sing itself. Waste not, want not. That's the way
Creative Writers learn to deal with it.
This is the way a poet handles shit.

Keeping it Clean

For Ric Hool.

Terminal Report. James Allen's Girls' School. 1954.
Needlework. Fair. Ann must try to keep her work clean.

It was a jacket for my brand new brother,
Made of a soft, cream-coloured flannelette.
A row of yellow silk embroidered ducks
with orange feet were marching round the hem,
stumbling across a ground of purple daisies,
their centres all picked out in knobby knots
for him to feel for with his little fingers.

The work was for him and because of him;
I needed him near it in the making.
Sometimes I would show him the work in progress;
He used to grab for it with his fat hands,
Kiss and bless it with formula and snot.

Miss H took it between finger and thumb.
Holding it away from her in a mime
Of overstated fastidiousness.
The work, she said, was more or less all right –
French seams, chain, stem and satin stitches - but
it was distinguished by the state of it
from the pristine handiwork of my peers.

I suppose from a purist's point of view
My work will always be a bit unclean.
It shows the signs of being carried round,
dumped on contaminated surfaces
and stained by contact with untidy life.

I have no artist's bridge to hold my hand
At a safe distance from the work itself;
I get my fingerprints all over it.

But look at it another way – how else
Could you be certain that the work was mine?

Little Room

Fifty springs are little room…
A E Housman

Bugger three score years and ten;
Yours truly is going for the ton.

Half way. Here I am, as it were, weighing things up.
Like Sisyphus taking a whiff at the top of the hill
Knowing that whether or not anything alters
Things are not going to stop as they are;
That the load I've pushed this far, thrutching against gravity,
Is going to go down again, whether I like it or not.

Well, then, it would seem that I have two choices.
Knowing that it's all going to go, I could turn my back to it,
Dig in my heels like a cartoon cat and let it shove me,
Red in the face with my four paws smoking and sparking
Down, back down to where I first put my shoulder against it.

Or

I could give it just one more little nudge and let it
Go bumpeting down the other side in advance of me.
I could follow it down at my leisure, stopping to pick cherries.
I could roll the stones on my tongue while I decided,
In my own sweet time, whether to spit or swallow.

A poem for myself, on having knocked up an undistinguished half century

Against Rhyming

*For U.A. Fanthorpe, who found me weeping on
the road to Jericho, having fallen among critics.*

"Rhyme gets you noticed". But it's just a flier
To get the punters near the proper stuff.
It's to free verse a poet should aspire;
Rhyming and chiming isn't strong enough
To carry messages of any weight
And real involvement in the here and now
Demands the rawness of the naked state
Of language. One can just imagine how
Imaginative thought would feel the pinch
Of being squeezed into a villanelle
Whose rigid metre wouldn't give an inch
When freedom's feet demanded space to swell.
Who in their right mind would contrive a sonnet
If anything worthwhile depended on it?

Double Dactyl

Rumpety Pumpety
Eros and Agape
Quelle opportunité!
Had to say yes

Sed in Arcadia
Minefield and mystery,
Megalomania –
Merde! What a mess!

Riverstation

The dog on the barge and the light on the river
And things understood and things unspoken
And the thought that this could go on forever –
The dog on the barge and the light on the river;
That if only I were sufficiently clever
The surface tension would stay unbroken,
The dog on the barge and the light on the river
And things understood and things unspoken.

Lines to a Gentleman,
On the gift of a Jigsaw Puzzle

After Herrick

Behold the box, rectangular and prim
Which doth belie the wantonness within.
A silken purse doth lurk beneath the lid
Wherein a puzzling paradox is hid.
A fistful of unprepossessing parts
To test dexterity of minds and hearts.
A host of little hollows and projections
Which at first sight do seem like imperfections
But which resolve in stages slow but sure
Into a sweet and seemly metaphor –

> A little patience and a little wit
> And see how all the little pieces fit!

From the Heart

Corinna's reply to the Earl of Rochester

Small liberties, if they be deftly taken,
Do such extreme of sweet delight awaken
That they do put to shame the greater act
As doth the poet's touch the unvarnished fact.
The meeting of like minds may thus discover
The bliss of bodies that amuse each other
And with compassion and good humour see
The simpler pleasures of maturity –
Of him who orchestrates his admiration
Without the urgency of procreation;
Of her whose greatest joy is to express
Desire's strength through wisdom's gentleness.
For them, the re-enactment of convention
Is sweetly spiced with exquisite invention
And while hot youth with ramrod haste discovers
The fleeting pleasure of more ardent lovers,
To me it seems the less insistent part
Doth move the swifter to engage my heart.

The Self I Made You

For D.G.

I made you an impressive self, my love.
From insufficient cloth I crafted it,
Stuffing you into it, dismissive of
The clear inadequacy of the fit.

I dreamed of you in it with me not there.
Forgive me, but I never thought you might
Slough it the moment you were out of sight;
Slip into something easier to wear.

Like a sad sweater knitted by an aunt
Of whom you weren't particularly fond,
You wore it bravely while I was around
And I was blind and deaf and innocent –
You looked so fetching in the fine disguise
I stitched together out of hope and lies.

New Fruit

In the last knockings of the evening sun
Eve drinks Calvados. Elsewhere in her life
She has played muse and mistress, bitch and wife.
Now all that gunpoint gamesmanship is done.
She loves the garden at this time of day.
Raising her third glass up to God, she grins;
If this is her come-uppance for her sins
It's worth a little angst along the way.
A fourth. Again the cork's slow squeaky kiss.
If, as the liquor tempts her to believe,
The Lord has one more Adam up His sleeve
He's going to have to take her as she is –
Out in the garden in a dressing-gown
Breathing old apples as the sun goes down.